UNIVER ... HAM
WIT ... N
ROM
D0258571

Oxford**basics**

TEACHING GRAMMAR

R

See the Oxford University Press ELT website at
http://www.oup.com/elt for further details.

Oxford**basics**

Teaching Grammar

JIM SCRIVENER

JUBILEE
CAMPUS
LRC

OXFORD
UNIVERSITY PRESS

OXFORD
UNIVERSITY PRESS

Great Clarendon Street, Oxford OX2 6DP

Oxford University Press is a department of the University
of Oxford. It furthers the University's objective of excellence
in research, scholarship, and education by publishing
worldwide in

Oxford New York

Auckland Bangkok Buenos Aires Cape Town Chennai
Dar es Salaam Delhi Hong Kong Istanbul Karachi Kolkata
Kuala Lumpur Madrid Melbourne Mexico City Mumbai Nairobi
São Paulo Shanghai Singapore Taipei Tokyo Toronto

Oxford and *Oxford English* are registered trade marks of
Oxford University Press in the UK and in certain other countries

© Oxford University Press 2003

The moral rights of the author have been asserted

Database right Oxford University Press (maker)

First published 2003

All rights reserved. No part of this publication may be
reproduced, stored in a retrieval system, or transmitted, in any
form or by any means, without the prior permission in writing
of Oxford University Press, or as expressly permitted by law
or under terms agreed with the appropriate reprographics
rights organization. Enquiries concerning reproduction outside
the scope of the above should be sent to the ELT Rights
Department, Oxford University Press, at the address above

You must not circulate this book in any other binding or cover
and you must impose this same condition on any acquirer

Photocopying

The publisher grants permission for the photocopying of those
pages marked 'photocopiable' according to the following
conditions. Individual purchasers may make copies for their
own use or for use by classes they teach. School purchasers
may make copies for use by staff and students, but this
permission does not extend to additional schools or branches

Under no circumstances may any part of this book be
photocopied for resale

Any websites referred to in this publication are in the public
domain and their addresses are provided by Oxford University
Press for information only. Oxford University Press disclaims any
responsibility for the content

ISBN 0 19 442179 1

Printed in China

Contents

Introduction

How can I teach grammar?

This book offers a wide range of answers to this question. The answers are especially directed to teachers in situations with limited resources. There is nothing here that needs more than a board and chalk. In fact, if you don't have even those things, you can probably still use most of the ideas here. At the most basic, the important resource is simply you, the teacher.

But before we look at teaching ideas, let's consider these important questions:

- What is grammar?
- Why learn grammar?
- How do learners learn grammar?
- How can I teach in a way that leads to effective learning?

What is grammar?

When thinking of 'grammar' many people probably imagine a book full of explanations and rules that tell them which verbs have what endings, how to use adverbs, how to make a superlative, etc. Certainly our learners need to know these things, but it isn't the information which is important – it's what they can do with it. We want learners to discover how to communicate using language. This kind of grammar is not just a dry list of facts and rules. It's in our heads and it's a living resource that gives us the ability to communicate our ideas and feelings and to understand what other people say or write to us.

So here's an important point – a learner who learns the rules in a grammar book by heart has not 'learnt grammar'. A teacher who gets learners to recite grammar rules by heart is not 'teaching grammar'. Except in exams, or related school situations, no-one will ever come up to a student and say 'Tell me about the Present perfect tense.' Grammar only makes any sense if you can use it.

Why learn grammar?

At a very basic level, words on their own are often enough to communicate with someone else. If I say to you, 'Plate. Food. Please.' and look as if I'm hungry and requesting something, you'll probably understand that I want you to give me some food. Other things can also help you understand what my meaning is, for example, the situation that we are in or what you know about me. However, when we want to express a more complex meaning, words on their own may not be enough.

So why do we use grammar? We use it to communicate more effectively, more precisely with others. That communication may be in a conversation or an essay or a notice or a hundred other things. We use grammar to 'fine-tune' a meaning, to make it more precise. A meaning such as 'I used to think about space a lot when I was a child' is hard to convey with individual words alone.

How do learners learn grammar?

It seems likely that learners need to do four things to be able to start making a new grammar item part of their own personal stock of language.

They need to:

- **notice** the item when it is being used, in texts, in stories, in conversation. It's very hard to learn a 'new' item the first time you are exposed to it. The more times you meet an item, the more likely it is to make sense to you. Plan for learners to be exposed to a grammar item a number of times as well as explicitly 'teaching' it.
- **understand** the *form* of an item, i.e. how it's made, how the pieces fit together, the endings, etc., its *meaning*, and its *use*, i.e. the typical situations, conversations, contexts in which it might be used.
- **try** things out in a safe environment. Learners need a lot of opportunities to practise new language. They probably won't even get the sounds or the words in the right order at the start. They might use it with a wrong meaning. Don't worry. That seems to be how humans learn. Learners probably need to get things wrong quite a few times before they get them right.
- **use** the new language when speaking and writing. Even after a lot of practice, it may still take a long time for newly studied language to become part of a learner's own language. Learners need opportunities to use the language in different situations, and they need to feel encouraged to take risks – sometimes getting things wrong and sometimes getting things right.

The answer to 'How do students learn grammar?' isn't a simple, easy one. Learning is quite a slow, messy business. It's better to acknowledge that, because then you won't come out of class angry with yourself and saying things like 'I taught it well but they didn't learn it.'

How can I *teach* in a way that leads to effective learning?

And here we are with the fourth and last question. Let's summarize where we've got to so far.

We want learners to be exposed to a lot of language. We need to help them notice it. We need to focus their attention on specific items so that they can understand what they mean, how they're formed, and when and where they are used. We need to give them a lot of opportunities to practise things in an encouraging environment, using the items when they speak and write.

That's it! How can you do it? That's what the rest of this book is about.

The book

Units in this book have the following:

- a brief introduction to a teaching technique
- a complete example lesson using the technique to demonstrate how it works
- at the back of the book an appendix with notes explaining the ideas behind each technique.

A time guide is given for each lesson, but remember that the actual length will vary depending on your teaching style and on factors such as how much you ask learners to speak and how much you extend the activities.

Use this book to generate your own lessons

This book introduces you to a range of grammar teaching techniques. But each example lesson shows only one way of using that technique – to get you thinking. So, don't only follow the lesson plans one by one; also think how you can apply the same techniques to different grammar points.

And remember – *everything* you do using English is 'grammar teaching'

As well as lessons that explicitly teach grammar, remember that everything you do in class using English is also providing language examples for learners to notice and learn from. You can help this process by creating a classroom environment rich in natural language learning possibilities, for example:

■ Use English yourself in class: This is probably the best input you can offer. All the time you speak English you're exposing learners to the language in use. Use English for instructions, for telling stories, for everything. Don't worry if the learners talk back to you in their language – just keep answering in English. Feel free to use the learners' own language when it's really necessary – just don't let it 'take over'.

■ Provide a library: One of the best ways for learners to acquire a large amount of language is for them to read. There's probably more language in one book than in a whole term's English lessons. And four or five books is enough to start a library. Put any suitable material into a small box and bring it to class with you whenever you come. You could include:
—readers – books written for learners
—reference books – encyclopaedias, science books, etc.
—magazines and newspapers, leaflets, brochures, etc.

Don't put in books like thick classics in unabridged English. It's better to have a small library with a few suitable things.

■ Fill the walls: Decorate the walls of the room you teach in. If you can't do the whole room, maybe do one wall, or a noticeboard. With what? Leaflets, posters, learners' stories and other writing, postcards, magazine pictures, interesting words in large letters, etc.

■ Chat: Don't feel you are wasting time if you have a five minute chat with the class at the start or end of a lesson. It's useful exposure – and may be the best source of natural language your class hears.

Activities

1 Listening and doing

TECHNIQUE You give your class simple instructions to do something. They then give similar instructions to each other.

LANGUAGE FOCUS Instructions using imperatives, for example, '*Walk* towards the door', '*Pick* up the book', '*Close* the door'.

LEVEL Elementary

RESOURCES A series of short instructions. Here is an example:

Walk to the door. Walk to the board. Walk back to the door. Open the door. Close the door. Walk back to the board. Pick up my book. Put down my book. Walk to Jorge's desk. Pick up Jorge's book. Open his book. Look at his book. Close his book. Put down the book. Pick up Jorge's book again. Give Jorge's book to Marinella. Pick up Marinella's pen. Give the pen to me. Thank you!

PREPARATION Prepare your instructions. You can make it longer or shorter to fit the lesson time and pace of the lesson. You can also vary the objects, for example, 'box' instead of 'book', 'pencil case' instead of 'pen', etc.

TIME GUIDE 30 minutes

....

Lesson

1 Ask a volunteer learner to come up to the front of the class. Read out your list of instructions sentence by sentence. Wait till the learner completes an action before you give the next instruction. If necessary, help them by pointing where to go, or by miming, etc. Make sure the rest of the class can see clearly. This should be a fun activity.

2 Ask a different learner to the front. Give the instructions again. Vary the instructions slightly, for example, 'pick up the book' instead of 'pick up the pen'. You could also change the sequence of instructions slightly and add in one or two new instructions. You can repeat the activity with a few more learners.

3 After five to ten minutes of this practice, ask the class if one of them would like to be the 'teacher'. If someone is keen to try, invite them to the front and let them give instructions to a learner in the same way you did. Help the 'teacher' by gently correcting any incorrect instructions they give. If there is no volunteer, continue with stage 2 until someone is ready.

4 Repeat stage 3 with more new 'teachers' and learners. One learner could give instructions for you to follow.

5 Draw four columns on the board. Write 'Walk' in the first column. Ask the class if they can remember which things people were asked to walk towards. As learners say 'door', 'desk', 'teacher', etc, write them in the fourth column. Ask the class which 'direction' words can go in the second column and which words can go in the third column. For example,

Walk	to	the	door.
	to	Jorge's	desk.
	up to	the	teacher.

6 Practise the pronunciation with the class. Read the following sentence, stressing the parts of the sentence marked with a dot.

$\quad\bullet\qquad\bullet\qquad\bullet$

Walk towards the door.

7 Ask learners to think of more items for the first column, for example, 'open', and 'pick'. Write them on the board as they suggest them. When you have all the verbs you used, ask the class to work in pairs and try to fill in the other columns of the grid, for example:

Open		*the*	*door.*
Pick	*up*	*Jorge's*	*book.*

Compare answers as a class when they have finished.

8 Ask learners to work individually to prepare a new list of instructions using their grid to help them. When learners are ready they should work in pairs (A and B). In each pair A reads out his/her instructions while B follows them. All pairs will be working simultaneously so there will be a quantity of noise, movement, and possibly some confusion! When A has finished, A and B should swap roles.

2 Using flashcards

TECHNIQUE	You use flashcards to help your learners understand new language and give the them interesting and challenging speaking practice.
LANGUAGE FOCUS	Things we count and don't count. See 'Resources' below.
LEVEL	Elementary
RESOURCES	Flashcards:

—things we count (countables): apples, pens, eggs, etc.
—things we don't count (uncountables): rice, sugar, tea, etc.
—things in containers (countable): a packet of crisps, a jar of coffee, etc.
—quantities of things (countable): a kilo of flour, a litre of milk, etc.
—a person with a shopping bag.

A piece of string and some clothes pegs.

The cards should be large enough for the whole class to see. You will need enough so that half the class have at least three or four cards for stage 6. The flashcards can be a mixture of pictures cut from magazines or newspapers and simple hand-drawn images. They can be reused.

PREPARATION	Prepare the flashcards as described above.
	Before the lesson, attach the string like a clothes line horizontally across the board using a drawing pin at each end.
TIME GUIDE	40 minutes

Lesson

1 Show the flashcard of the person. Introduce him or her to the class, for example, 'This is Chen.' Tell them that he is going into town to do some shopping. Say, 'He wants to buy …' and hold up a flashcard of a countable item, for example, 'a pen'. Ask the class what is on the card and say the sample sentence, 'He wants to buy a

pen.' Ask the class to repeat it. Do the same thing with 'apples', then things in containers, quantities of things, something we don't count, for example:

He wants to buy a jar of coffee, a kilogram of flour, some tea, etc.

2 Keep showing new cards and eliciting new sentences. Reshow cards occasionally to revise answers. After a while you'll need to say much less yourself – aim to get to the point where you can show a card and the class will correctly say the sentence themselves.

3 Use your clothes line and pegs to hang the first card on the board. Hang countables on the left and uncountables on the right.

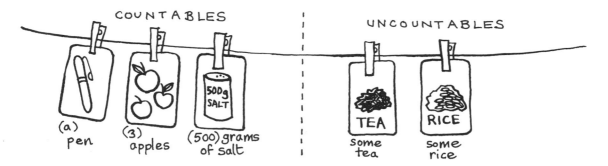

Elicit and then write the name of the item under it. Ask the class if they can remember how much Chen wanted. Write this amount on the board below the item. Continue hanging more cards in the same way.

4 Show the rest of the cards more quickly, one by one, asking the class to decide which side of the board they should go on, and peg them up.

5 Divide the class into two halves – one half of shop assistants and the other of shoppers. Tell the shoppers to write a shopping list (name and quantity) using only items that were on the flashcards. Distribute the flashcards randomly among the shop assistants.

6 Tell the shoppers they can now go shopping. They stand up with their shopping list and go to a 'shop', where they ask for items on their lists, for example, 'Could I have some tea, a litre of milk, three apples?'. If the shop assistant has a flashcard with the requested item, the shopper can cross that item off their list. After 'shopping' at one 'store' they can then move on and meet someone else. Allow enough time for learners to go to a few shops. At the end find out if anyone has managed to find everything on their shopping list. The class could then play the game again, swapping the two roles.

3 Using dialogues 1 – acting

TECHNIQUE	You introduce new language to your class by helping them to act out and remember a short dialogue.
LANGUAGE FOCUS	'Any' in questions with countable and uncountable nouns.
LEVEL	Elementary
RESOURCES	A dialogue, for example:

ANNIE *Hey, Sally. What are you doing in my kitchen?*
SALLY *I'm cooking supper for you.*
ANNIE *Great!*
SALLY *Have you got any flour?*
ANNIE *Half a kilo. Is that enough?*
SALLY *Yes. (Pours flour into bowl) And milk. Is there any milk?*
ANNIE *I think so. Yes. Two litres.*
SALLY *(Pours milk into bowl and stirs) Any sugar? Any eggs?*
ANNIE *Yup. A packet of sugar. Three eggs.*
SALLY *(Adds sugar. Breaks eggs. Stirs.) Have you got any chocolate?*
ANNIE *Yes. But what are you making?*
SALLY *Chocolate pancakes! OK?*
ANNIE *Great!*

PREPARATION	Choose a learner who can help you act out the dialogue. This person should be one of the more confident learners in your class. Briefly tell him or her what they will need to do.
	If you don't use the example dialogue, you can prepare your own. Make sure it sounds realistic for your area.
TIME GUIDE	30 minutes

Lesson

1 Invite your helper to the front. Tell the class that you are going to act out a conversation. They must decide where it is, who is in it, and what they are talking about. Write 'Where?', 'Who?', and 'What?' on the board to remind them of the questions.

You and the helper mime the conversation without saying anything, i.e. Annie coming in and looking surprised, asking questions, Sally pouring, breaking eggs, stirring, etc. Ask the class the 'Where?', 'Who?', and 'What?' questions. Make sure everyone understands that the conversation takes place in a kitchen, there are two friends, and one of them is cooking supper.

2 Say that you are going to mime the first four sentences again. Ask the class to watch and guess what the words are. Mime the first four lines again with the helper. When the class have suggested what the actual words are, act out the first four lines again, this time aloud so that the class can check if they were right.

3   Ask the class to repeat the first four lines and then ask them to guess the rest of the dialogue as you and your helper mime. Draw prompts on the board to help:

When they have guessed the first half of the dialogue, get the class to practise the first half of the dialogue in pairs. Then continue in the same way with the second half of the dialogue.

4   Thank your helper and ask them to sit down. Ask the class if they can recall the whole dialogue, and as they do write it up on the board. When it is complete ask the class to copy the dialogue into their books.

5   When they have finished, ask learners to close their books. Go to the dialogue on the board and erase some keywords, e.g. 'doing', 'cooking', 'supper', 'flour', 'kilo', 'milk', 'litres', 'sugar' 'eggs', 'making', 'chocolate', and 'pancakes'. Ask all the pairs to try to recall the whole dialogue without looking at their books.

6   Divide the class into new groups of three. Explain that two of them are 'actors' and one of them is a 'director'. Give the groups five minutes to discuss and think of some alternative words to put instead of the erased words, in order to make a new dialogue. It's not necessary to change everything. For example:

LEARNER 1   *What are you doing?*
LEARNER 2   *I'm making breakfast. Have you got any cornflakes?*

Walk round and check that the new scripts are correct. When they are ready give the learners five minutes to find the best way of acting their scene. The director can set up the scene, give advice, etc.

7   After ten minutes, stop them and invite pairs to watch each other's dialogue. Walk round and give them encouragement. You could also invite one or two pairs to perform in front of the class. Give feedback if any of the pairs still have problems using 'any' correctly.

4 Using pictures 1 – situations

TECHNIQUE
You use pictures to illustrate typical situations in which the language is used. The pictures can also prompt your learners to use the language.

LANGUAGE FOCUS
Present progressive to talk about activities that are happening at present, for example, 'She's dancing.'

LEVEL
Elementary

RESOURCES
This picture on the blackboard:

These 6 smaller pictures on paper:

Some sticky tape or board magnets.

A conversation script based on the picture, making use of the target language items.

PREPARATION
Practise drawing the main picture and decide the board layout. Prepare the smaller pictures on medium-sized pieces of paper.

TIME GUIDE
30 minutes

Lesson

1 Draw the large picture on the board. Label the two people as 'Colin' and 'Barbara' (or names of your choice). Ask questions to establish the situation, for example:

12

How many people are there in the picture? (Two.)
Where is the man?   (At home.)
Where is the woman?   (At a party.)
What are they doing?   (They're speaking to each
                                             other on the phone.)
What do you think they're talking about?   (The party.)

Stick all the smaller pictures at random under the big picture. Tell the class to listen to the conversation between Colin and Barbara. Read the conversation aloud in a natural way:

BARBARA   *Barbara speaking.*
COLIN   *Hello, Barbara. How's the party?*
BARBARA   *Hi, Colin. It's great!*
COLIN   *What's Emma doing?*
BARBARA   *She's dancing!*

Ask the class to choose the appropriate picture (woman dancing) and attach it to the board under the 'Party' sign in the big picture. Repeat the question about Emma and the answer. Then ask the class 'What's Emma doing?' and help them answer it correctly. Get someone in the class to ask another learner the question. Check that the question and answer are correct.

2   Ask the class to listen to the next part of the conversation. This time read:

'What's Mike doing?'
'He's talking to a girl.'

As before, ask the class to choose a picture and get the class to listen and repeat the answer. Do the same again with the other pictures.

3   Recap the whole conversation by pointing at each picture one by one. See if the learners can remember the question and answer for each one. With the learners' help, write the dialogue on the board and give them time to copy it down.

4   Ask a learner to 'phone' someone across the classroom and have a conversation like the one you wrote up. When that has finished, divide the class into pairs and get them to phone each other. Encourage them to add new ideas to the dialogue.

5 Creating imaginary situations

TECHNIQUE	You set up short, imaginary scenes in class to provide your class with memorable contexts for learning new language.
LANGUAGE FOCUS	'Can' and 'can't', for example, 'He can stand on one foot', 'He can't pick up the car.'
LEVEL	Elementary
RESOURCES	Classroom objects; a toy or model of an elephant or other objects.
PREPARATION	Choose two confident learners for stage 2. Write 'OLYMPICS' in big letters on the board.
	Put a few small objects on your desk, for example, a pen and a toy elephant or similar object.
TIME GUIDE	30 minutes

Lesson

1 Pretend you are a TV announcer speaking into a microphone and say 'Ladies and Gentlemen. Welcome to the (year) Olympics. We are going to choose the (your location) Olympic champion. To become champion they must pass the Olympic test.'

2 Ask the learners you chose to come to the front of the class. Say to one learner, 'Contestant number one, can you stand on one foot for a minute?' If he/she does this successfully, encourage a round of applause and call out 'Congratulations! Contestant one can stand on one foot for a minute.' Ask the class to repeat your sentence once or twice, and maybe drill some individual learners.

Repeat the same procedure with contestant two. Then introduce contestant three – yourself. Pretend to try the same challenge as the learners, but fail to stand on one foot for any length of time (wobbling, overbalancing, etc.).

Announce 'Oh dear, contestant three can't stand on one foot for a minute.' Get the class to repeat this.

3 Ask two new contestants to come to the front. Ask them to do a new 'test', for example, 'Hold your breath for 30 seconds'. Repeat the same procedure as stage 2. Do the same with new contestants each time and the following 'tests': 'touch your toes', 'walk with a book on your head', 'touch your nose with your tongue', 'stand a pen on your fingertip', 'pick up an elephant', etc. Each time fail to do the test yourself as contestant three.

4 Write these sentences on the board, without the stress marks, and ask the class to copy them:

•   •   •

Contestant three   can't   pick up   an elephant.

•   •   •   •

Contestant two   can   stand   on one foot for a minute.

Tell learners you are going to read the sentences and ask them to tell you which words you stress. Add the stress marks to the sentences.

Explain that 'can't' is stressed in the first sentence, and the verb is stressed in the second sentence – 'can' is not stressed. Give the class practice with the two sentences. Ask if anyone can suggest more sentences from the 'Olympics' and write them on the board.

5 Show learners how they can ask and answer questions. Write up some examples:

Can	*you*	*stand*	*on one foot for a minute?*
		pick	*up an elephant?*
Yes,	*I*	*can.*	
No,	*I*	*can't.*	

6 Divide the class into TV presenters and Olympic contestants. Demonstrate the role play by asking one learner some questions from the sentences on the board, for example, 'Can you touch your toes?' The learner must answer 'Yes, I can' or 'No, I can't' and show that they can or can't do the action.

When you have demonstrated one or two questions, divide the class into pairs and get them to do the role play in the same way. If your class is confident, they could extend the role play by introducing more questions.

6 Using information gaps

<dl>
<dt>TECHNIQUE</dt>
<dd>Your learners have different pieces of information. They practise their communication skills by sharing the information in a speaking activity.</dd>

<dt>LANGUAGE FOCUS</dt>
<dd>Prepositions of place: on, under, inside, next to, on top of, beside, between, etc.

Kitchen vocabulary: shelves, fridge, cupboard, table, etc.</dd>

<dt>LEVEL</dt>
<dd>Elementary</dd>

<dt>RESOURCES</dt>
<dd>A picture of a kitchen – it could look like the one below or adapted to look like a kitchen in your area.</dd>
</dl>

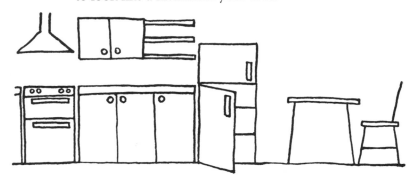

<dl>
<dt>PREPARATION</dt>
<dd>Practise drawing the kitchen picture.</dd>

<dt>TIME GUIDE</dt>
<dd>40 minutes</dd>
</dl>

Lesson

1 Draw the picture of the kitchen on the board and ask the learners to copy it. Tell them to use a whole page. You could use this drawing time as an opportunity to check kitchen vocabulary.

2 Use the board picture to teach learners some prepositions of place. Draw a few simple objects, for example, an apple, some cheese, a plate, a pan, a bottle, etc., in various places and help learners to say where they are, for example, 'It's on the top shelf', 'It's under the table', etc.

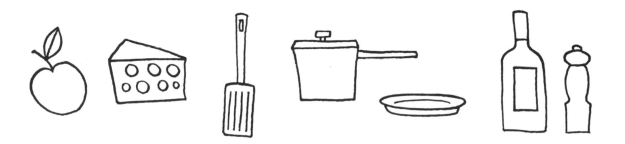

Make sure everyone in the class adds these objects to their own kitchen picture in the correct position exactly as it is on the board. Go through these locations in the kitchen picture:

It's	*on the bottom/top/first/ second/third*	*shelf*
	on/on top of/under/ next to/beside	*the table/fridge/cooker the cup/can/cheese*
	in/inside	*the oven/fridge*
	between	*the cooker and the shelves/the table and the fridge*

3 Show the class how to draw a mouse. Ask each learner to draw three mice somewhere in the picture – secretly! Demonstrate by drawing a mouse on the table (in the board picture). Learners must not let the others see their picture.

4 Tell them that your Aunt Hannah has lots of mice everywhere. She has asked the class to help her find them. Demonstrate the activity to the class by taking your own room picture on a piece of paper and playing the game with one learner in front of the class.

Divide the class into pairs, sitting so that they cannot see their partner's drawing. They then exchange information with each other to find out where the three mice are. Tell them that when they have found exactly where a mouse is, they should add it in their own picture.

5 When the activity is over, you can give some feedback. Take the chance to help them with any language they had problems with, especially prepositions.

6 After this, repeat the information gap activity. Apart from your example mouse, the learners now have six mice in their pictures, their own three, and another three from their partner. Ask them to work with a new partner and do the same game again, this time explaining where *six* mice are. This will provide some very useful consolidation of the work done. You'll probably find they use language a lot better second time round.

7 Doing role plays

TECHNIQUE	You provide your class with a framework to create and develop role plays.
LANGUAGE FOCUS	'Will' (short form '-ll') in spontaneous offers of help and promises, for example, 'I'll do it!'
LEVEL	Lower intermediate
RESOURCES	A role play preparation grid:

	1	2	3
Who are you?			
Who are you talking to?			
Where are you?			
What are you talking about?			

PREPARATION	None
TIME GUIDE	40 minutes

Lesson

1 Teach 'will' and ''ll' as used in offers and promises by using board pictures (as in Unit 4) to create the following context:

A student has left his/her school bag at home so he/she doesn't have any pens, or sweater, or lunch box, etc. His/her friend offers to help. Explain that we use 'will'/''ll' when we offer someone help, for example, 'I'll lend you mine'.

2 Write the preparation grid on the board and ask learners to copy it.

3 Divide the class into pairs – one person taking role A, the other role B. They should write their roles in the grid, for example:

Role A		Role B	
	1		*1*
Who are you?	*Friend with no bag*	*Who are you?*	*Friend*
Who are you talking to?	*Friend*	*Who are you talking to?*	*Friend with no bag*

4   Ask the class to help you fill in the other column 1 boxes on the board as below and ask the learners to copy them, for example:

Where are you?	*at school*
What are you talking about?	*friend's problems – no books, pens, food, sweater, etc.*

5   Tell the pairs that they should now have a conversation between the two people. The first friend will say problems she/he has; the other friend will offer to help. Remind them of how to make offers before they start. When they've finished get feedback on what they talked about. Collect some correct sentences on the board.

6   Use the 'preparation grid' again. This time one person will role play an old person with heavy bags at a station, the other person a tourist. Again let them choose who is who and write 'old person' or 'tourist' in the correct places in column two. Fill in the rest of column two with the other information about the situation, for example, 'Where are you?' could be a 'railway station'. They could be talking about 'carrying bags', 'buying a ticket', 'getting on a train', etc. When the learners are ready they can try this new conversation.

7   Afterwards ask learners to think of a third situation where someone makes offers similar to the first two role plays. They will discuss their ideas in their pairs and fill column three in themselves. This time you will get a wide range of different role plays. It might be good to see some of the most interesting ones performed up at the front of the class. If you have time, you could also do a fourth role play in the same way.

8 Using a diary

TECHNIQUE
You use a diary to explain a grammar point. Afterwards you use the same diary as an information gap activity and your learners compare diary entries with each other.

LANGUAGE FOCUS
'Going to' to talk about future plans.

LEVEL
Lower intermediate

RESOURCES
A blank diary frame starting from the day of the lesson. Here is an example:

	Friday	Saturday	Sunday	Monday
morning				
afternoon				
evening				

An explanation of your plans, for example:

> Today I'm going to work at school all day. This evening at seven I'm going to play football. Tomorrow morning I'm going to walk to the market and I'm going to buy a CD. In the afternoon I'm going to meet my friend Peter. On Sunday I'm going to stay at home and listen to music.

PREPARATION
Prepare your explanation for stage 2.

TIME GUIDE
40 minutes

Lesson

1   Draw the diary frame on the board.

2   Tell the class about your plans for the next few days. As you state each plan add a brief entry to the diary, for example, 'market', 'Peter', etc. If necessary, help the learners to understand by miming actions, for example, shaking hands for 'meeting', or drawing little pictures, for example, a football, a CD. It may be worth repeating all the sentences a few times.

3   Ask the class to tell you your schedule using the word and picture prompts. Mime the actions again if they need help. Encourage them to use 'going to'.

4 'Write up these substitution tables and ask the class to copy them:

What are you going to do	tonight?	I'm going to	play football.
What's he going to do	tomorrow?	He's going to	meet Peter.
What's she going to do	on Saturday? on Sunday morning?	She's going to She's going to	go to the market. buy a cassette.

Ask the class if the sentences are about the past, present, or future. Ask if there is a small chance you will do the things or if they are definite plans. (Answer: They are definite plans for the future.)

5 Ask learners to copy the blank diary into their books; make sure it is large enough to allow them to write in the spaces. Ask learners to think about what they are going to do in the next four days and fill in their diary.

6 Put the class into pairs and tell them to find out what their partner is planning to do without looking at the other person's diary. They should write the information into their diary, for example, if Idris says he is going to catch a bus to his village, the partner could write 'Idris – bus' in their diaries.

7 Rearrange the pairs so everyone is working with a new partner. Using their diary to remind them, learners tell their new partners what their previous partners are planning to do, for example, 'On Sunday Idris is going to catch a bus to his village. He's going to visit his family.'

8 Finally, the first and third pairs should find the partner they heard about and check that they got the right information, for example, 'Idris, are you going to visit your village on Sunday?'

9 Reading a story

TECHNIQUE
You give the class a story to read which contains examples of the target language.

LANGUAGE FOCUS
'Going to' to refer to the future, for example, 'I'm going to have a swim.'

LEVEL
Lower intermediate

RESOURCES
A reading passage about 300 words long. The passage should be just slightly above the general current level of the class, i.e. they don't need to know every piece of vocabulary or every grammatical item. Here is an example text:

Lee was walking along the old road to the market to meet his mother. He stopped to have a rest and saw an old lady drinking tea.
'Hi,' called the lady. 'What's up?'
'Oh, it's just too hot! I'm going to see my mother at the market. Then I'm going to get home out of the sun.'
'I know a good place to cool down,' said the old lady. 'There's a beautiful lake on the other side of this hill. I'm going to have a swim there.'
Now, Lee had lived in the area all his life. There was no lake on the other side of the hill, just an old factory. He thought she must be a little crazy.
'Are you going to come and see it?' asked the old lady. 'It's not far.'
'OK,' replied Lee. 'Why not?' He was curious to see what the old lady was talking about. They walked till finally the path came round the hill and Lee saw the other side. He was amazed. There was a beautiful, cool green lake, surrounded by tall trees. He tried to ask the old lady a question, but she was already walking towards the water.
'I'm going to swim,' called the lady. 'Maybe you can come and swim here one day.'
'But I want to swim now,' said Lee, rather puzzled.
'Maybe not yet, young man. You are going to meet your mother at the market, aren't you?'
The old lady walked slowly into the water, smiling.
As she started swimming, Lee felt his head spinning. The lake looked smaller. The trees looked shorter. He closed his eyes for a second and when he opened them, there was no lake, no trees, no old lady. All he could see was the old factory – a large oily puddle on the ground and the tall factory chimneys. He walked slowly back around the hill. It was a very hot day.

PREPARATION
Copy your chosen text enough times so that there's one copy between two or three learners.

TIME GUIDE
40 minutes

Lesson

1 Tell the learners to gather round the texts so that everyone can see one clearly. Before the learners start reading set one or two questions about the general meaning of the text so that they have a specific goal when they are reading, for example:

How many people are there in the story? (two)
What was the weather like? (very hot)
In the story who walks and who swims? (Lee and the old lady walk; only the old lady swims)

2 Let learners read and then discuss the answers together. If you are satisfied that they have a basic idea of the text, set questions on more detailed points and let them read the text again to find the answers, for example:

What is Lee going to do? (He's going to meet his mother.)
What is he going to do after that? (He's going to go home.)
What is the old lady going to do? (She's going to have a swim.)

3 Ask learners for their own ideas about the passage, for example:

'Is the lake really there?'
'What happens to the old lady?'

4 Next ask learners to look at the text and see how many times they can find 'going to'. Ask the class these questions:

—Do the sentences refer to the past or the future?
—Do they refer to something that Lee or the old lady have already decided to do?

Take time over this stage and let the learners discuss and notice how the language is used. At the end, ask learners to turn over the texts.

5 Ask them how many 'going to' sentences they can remember. In pairs they should work on recalling and writing them without looking again at the texts.

6 Ask pairs to call out their sentences. Whether they are correct or not, write them up on the board as they say them. Write up errors without comment. When you have collected all the sentences ask learners to look again at the texts to check if what is on the board is correct.

7 Ask learners to predict the next part of the story. What is going to happen next?

10 Using dialogues 2 – noticing

TECHNIQUE	You give your learners a dialogue which helps them to notice how the target language is used.
LANGUAGE FOCUS	Contrasting uses of the present continuous and 'will' to talk about the future. For example, 'I'm meeting Garcia.' vs. 'I'll meet you at Garcia's.'
LEVEL	Lower intermediate
RESOURCES	A short dialogue that includes examples of the language items you want to focus on. For example:

ROB   *Would you like any more food?*

BELINDA   *No thanks. That was delicious. **Are you doing** anything tonight?*

ROB   *I**'m working** at the club till ten. Then I**'m going** home. What about you?*

BELINDA   *Oh, I don't know. Maybe I**'ll go** to the cinema. No, I know. I**'ll go** round and see Garcia.*

ROB   *I'd like to see Garcia too.*

BELINDA   *Great!*

ROB   *OK. I**'ll meet** you at Garcia's after the club.*

PREPARATION	Write out two copies of the dialogue. Show them to two confident learners before the lesson.
TIME GUIDE	40 minutes

Lesson

1 Write 'Where?' and 'Who?' on the board. Tell the class that they will listen to a short conversation and they should decide where the people are and who they are. These questions are intended to get the learners to listen carefully and get a general idea of the meaning of the conversation.

2 Ask the two confident learners to the front and perform the dialogue. Ask the class for possible answers to the two questions you put on the board. There are no fixed 'correct' answers, though it's probable that the two people are friends and they are in A's home, having lunch together.

3 Tell the class that they will listen to the dialogue twice again. This time they should try to make a note of ways people talk about the future. These are in bold in the dialogue. Ask the learners to act the dialogue twice more. When they've finished, ask the class to compare their answers in pairs.

4 Ask the learners for their suggestions and encourage them to try and tell you the exact sentences used to talk about the future in the

dialogue. Write their suggestions on the board and elicit corrections if there are any errors.

5 Write these two headings, 'Decisions made before the conversation' and 'Decisions made during the conversation' on the board. Check the class understand the difference between the two with the questions, 'What activities did they decide to do before the conversation? Which activities did they decide to do during the conversation?' Ask the class to tell you which sentences go under which heading, i.e.

Decisions made before the conversation	Decisions made during the conversation
(Are you doing anything tonight?) I'm working at the club. I'm going home.	Maybe I'll go to the cinema. I'll go round and see Garcia. I'll meet you at Garcia's.

6 Explain the following new situation to the class:

Two people talking about plans for their summer holidays. One person has a plan, the other person hasn't.

Write the first few lines of the dialogue on the board:

ANNA   *Have you got any plans for the summer holiday?*
CHRIS   *Yes, I've got lots of ideas!*
ANNA   *Oh, dear. I haven't got any . . .*

Ask the class to continue the conversation. The Chris character has already made his decisions and the Anna character makes decisions during the conversation. For example,

CHRIS   *I'm visiting my relatives in the country.*
ANNA   *That's a good idea. Maybe I'll visit my aunt.*

11 Making questionnaires

TECHNIQUE	You help your class create questionnaires which they use to interview each other.
LANGUAGE FOCUS	Present perfect for experiences, for example, 'Have you ever …?', 'I've never …'.
LEVEL	Lower intermediate
RESOURCES	Two questionnaires – the second questionnaire should use the same verbs as the first, but with different nouns. These examples focus on present perfect questions:

Questionnaire 1 – 'Have you ever …?' – 'Yes, I have.' / 'No, I haven't.'

Names	1	2	3
played basketball?			
caught a fish?			
been to the capital of your country?			
tasted a fresh pineapple?			
seen a parrot?			
walked 10 kilometres?			
done a jigsaw?			

Questionnaire 2

Names	1	2	3
played chess?			
caught a mouse?			
been to the seaside?			
tasted a fresh mango?			
seen a helicopter?			
walked in a forest?			
done a crossword?			

PREPARATION	Design your questionnaires. Write the first questionnaire on the board before the lesson. You can adapt the questions to fit the location and the class.
TIME GUIDE	40 minutes

Lesson

1 Check the class understand the phrase 'played basketball' by miming the action, drawing a little picture, showing a prepared flashcard, or translating. Draw the time line on the board. Ask one of the learners the first question, for example, 'Viktoria. Have you ever played basketball?' If her answer is 'Yes', use the diagram to point out that we don't know when she played – just that it was something in the past.

Explain that the question 'Have you ever ...?' refers to an experience or experiences in the past.

2   Write 'Yes' next to the first question on the questionnaire and ask the learner the rest of the questions. Write the answer on the questionnaire each time.

3   Explain that we have heard what one learner thinks. Now you would like to find out what everyone thinks. Erase key words from the board questionnaire and substitute the alternative words from your questionnaire number two. Ask the learners to copy the whole questionnaire. Make sure they leave enough space to write answers in. If it is a strong, confident class, you could leave some spaces in the table and get the learners to suggest two or three similar questions to add themselves.

4   Tell the learners to work with another person and write his/her name at the top of column 1. They must ask their partner questions and write answers in the correct place, putting 'Yes' or 'No'.

5   When the learners have finished with one person, they should move around and ask a new person, this time filling in column 2, then a third person for column 3.

6   When the class has finished, get some feedback – ask the class if they found any interesting answers. They should now be using the he/she forms of the verbs and may need an explanation about the third person 'has'. You can write a table like this on the board if they seem to be having problems:

| Peri | has | seen | a helicopter. |
| Cecilia | hasn't | played | chess. |

7   If you think the class would benefit from further practice, you could ask them to design their own questionnaire. Walk round the class helping and correcting where necessary. The class then repeat stages 4 and 5.

12 Telling a story

TECHNIQUE	You tell a true or nearly true personal story so that your learners can hear examples of the target language in an interesting and motivating context.
LANGUAGE FOCUS	Using the Past simple: 'was' and 'were'.
LEVEL	Elementary
RESOURCES	Write a short story about your life including some examples of the target language and some interesting or funny personal details. You could invent these details if you want to, though it's usually more interesting if the events you describe are true.

Here is an example of one teacher's story. It includes lots of examples of 'was' and 'were'.

This is a story about when I was a schoolboy. It was my 12th birthday but only my aunt was home. My parents were away for a month in another town. I was quite sad about this – no party!

After school I came home and it was very strange. The house door was open. The house was quiet. Every room was empty. But there was something interesting in my bedroom. In the middle of the floor was a big box. Inside was … a bike. It was wonderful. I took the bike outside – and everyone was there – all my friends. And my mum and dad were outside … laughing. It was fantastic.

PREPARATION	Prepare your own story.

Select about nine or ten key words or phrases from the story, i.e. the most important words from a story – usually the nouns, verbs, and adjectives. In this example story the key words and phrases might be: 'schoolboy', 'birthday', 'parents', 'sad', 'party', 'open', 'box', 'bike', and 'laughing'.

TIME GUIDE	40 minutes

. . . .

Lesson

1   In class, write three or four of the key words and phrases on the board in the wrong order, for example, 'bike', 'laughing', 'box', 'schoolboy'. Explain that these words are from a story about your life. Ask the class to look at the words and guess what the story is about. Give them a minute to discuss in pairs, then invite some to tell their ideas to the whole class. Don't tell them if they are right or wrong.

2   Add the rest of the words to the board, again in mixed-up order. Give the class some more time to discuss and see if they can think of the story. Again you can ask them to share their ideas, and again, don't let them know if they are close or not.

3 Say 'Now I'm going to tell you my story. Listen and see if your story is right.' Tell the story in an interesting way. Don't just read it aloud. At the end, let them discuss whose prediction was closest to your story.

4 Point at the list of words on the board. Ask the class which word came first. Write '1' next to the word the class suggest. Divide the class into pairs and get them to number all the other words in the order they think they came in the story. This task encourages the students to try and remember the story, the sequence of events, and some of the language you used.

5 When they are ready with their answers tell them to listen and check. Tell your story again. Let the class compare who got the best answer. If necessary, you can tell your story a third time.

6 Write your whole story on the board, but leave out the 'was' and 'were' verbs. Ask the class to copy it and write the correct words in the spaces. Don't tell them all the words are 'was' or 'were' – let them work out what is possible for the spaces.

7 Check the answers together, then ask questions about the language:

'Why did I use the word 'was', not 'is'?' (Because the story is about the past.)

'What is the difference between 'was' and 'were'?' (We use 'was' with 'I', 'he', 'she', 'it', and singular nouns; we use 'were' with 'we', 'you' 'they' and plural nouns, e.g. 'people'.)

Pointing at 'was' and 'were' – 'How do you pronounce these words in a sentence?', for example, 'I was quite sad.' 'My parents were away.' (The 'a' sound in 'was' and the first 'e' sound in 'were' are not stressed.)

8 Write up this framework story and ask learners to copy it, including the blank spaces. When they have written it they should add words of their choice to make a new story of their own. Afterwards learners can read their stories to each other.

Last year I was _____ years old. One day I was in/at _____ . I was very _____. I met _____. He / she was very _____. He / she said, '_____'.

I said, '_____'. I was there for _____ hours. Then I went home and my parents were very _____ because I was _____.

13 Using pictures 2 – stories

TECHNIQUE	You show your class a sequence of pictures and encourage them to recreate the story in words.
LANGUAGE FOCUS	Past simple regular and irregular verbs.
LEVEL	Lower intermediate
RESOURCES	A short story between 5 and 10 sentences long that includes examples of the target language, in this case, the Past simple. The story should have a clear sequence of events and should be a story that you can tell clearly with pictures. Here is an example:

*One morning Joan **was** in the kitchen doing the washing.*
*She **put** down the washing basket next to the washing machine.*
*She **heard** the phone and **went** into the living room.*
*While she was talking the cat **came** into the kitchen and **got** into the basket.*
*Joan **came** back and **put** the washing into the machine.*
*When she **came** back later she **saw** the cat in the machine!*

Plan some simple pictures that you can use to tell the story. Prepare the pictures on separate sheets of paper before the lesson. Use thick pens so that the pictures can be seen easily from the back of the room.

PREPARATION	You need to prepare the story and the pictures.
TIME GUIDE	40 minutes

. . . .

Lesson   **1**   Use sticky tape to stick the first picture on the top-left of the blackboard. Encourage learners to tell the first part of the story. Help them by asking questions, for example:

What is this? – It's a washing machine.
What is the person's name? – (Joan).
What did she do? – She put the washing down.
Where? – Next to the washing machine.
etc.

Don't write any sentences on the board – part of the challenge is getting learners to remember them.

2   Stick the next picture up on the board to the right of the first picture. Ask questions and elicit ideas and sentences in the same way as you did with picture one. Continue in the same way with the other pictures. Get the class to practise telling the story in pairs.

3   Ask the class if they can remember all the Past simple verbs in the story (they are in bold in the example). They should work in pairs, writing down a list of all the ones they can recall. The pictures on the board can help them.

4   When they have finished let them first check with other pairs to see if their lists are the same. Then say 'I'm going to read the whole story to you. Listen and check your list of verbs.' Tell the story using either your original text or the learners' own version.

5   Ask the learners to help you write the story. Pick up your chalk and tell them 'I am a writing robot.' You may need to explain the idea of a robot in their language. 'I will write everything you tell me to write. Tell me the story.' When a learner suggests a sentence from the story write up exactly what they say including mistakes.

6   If a learner suggests a sentence with a mistake in it, ask them, 'Are you happy with this sentence? Is there anything you'd like to change?' Continue helping them to find the mistake with other questions, for example, 'Is the verb OK?', 'Is it in the past simple?', 'Does it fit the subject?', etc. If the learner can't find the mistake, ask the class to help.

7   Continue till the end of the story. When the whole story is complete, the class can copy it down in their books.

14 Dictating keywords

TECHNIQUE	You provide your learners with the words they need to recreate a story.
LANGUAGE FOCUS	Regular and irregular Past simple verbs.
LEVEL	Lower intermediate
RESOURCES	A short story that includes about 15–20 verbs in the Past simple. The following is an example:

*Sylvia **went** to the market because her mum **wanted** some fruit. She **bought** some apples and oranges. But then unfortunately she **knocked over** a very large melon which **fell** onto a box. The box **broke** and a chicken **escaped**. It **ran away** down the street and Sylvia **chased after** it but she **couldn't catch** it. Then the chicken **jumped** onto a bus! So Sylvia **followed** it. Finally, inside the bus she **caught** the chicken. When the bus **stopped** Sylvia and the chicken **got off**. She **felt** happy until she **looked** around. She **was** completely lost!*

PREPARATION	Write the dictation text. When the story is ready, list all the past verbs separately with numbers, for example:

1 went	7 escaped	13 caught
2 wanted	8 ran away	14 stopped
3 bought	9 chased after	15 got off
4 knocked over	10 couldn't catch	16 felt
5 fell	11 jumped	17 looked
6 broke	12 followed	18 was

TIME GUIDE	40 minutes

Lesson

1 Tell the learners that you will dictate 18 verbs and explain that they should write down the words with correct spelling. Read through the list of words, making sure you allow sufficient time for the learners to write them down. It may help to repeat each word two or three times.

2 When you've finished ask the class to get into pairs and compare their lists. They should see if they have the same words and the same spelling.

3 When the pairs have finished checking together, check the answers with the whole class. Get the learners to dictate the list back to you while you write it on the board. You can ask them to spell some difficult words. They can get some practice with the pronunciation of the alphabet here as well.

4 When the whole list is on the board correctly, tell them that these are all words from one story and the words come in exactly the same order in the story. The learners will now work in pairs to make a story that has all 18 verbs in that order. They are not trying to guess your story, but to make a new story themselves. They can add other verbs and language, but must include the 18 verbs in exactly the form and order you dictated them in.

Emphasize that they should discuss the story rather than write it down, otherwise they'll become focused entirely on a piece of paper in front of them. This stage may take up to 15 minutes.

5 When they have finished, join two pairs together to make groups of four. The pairs tell the other pair their story. Walk around and listen in. Aim to enjoy the stories, rather than correct or help. If the learners seem to enjoy this, you could re-mix the pairs later so they can hear more stories.

6 You won't have time to hear all the stories when the whole class comes back together, but it may be nice to hear one or two.

7 They'll probably want to know what your story is. Tell them the story in an interesting way, but try not to give the impression that this is the 'right' answer.

15 Miming

TECHNIQUE   You mime and encourage your learners to describe what you are doing.

LANGUAGE FOCUS   Past progressive + 'when' or 'and' + Past simple, for example, 'I was watching TV when the power went off.'

LEVEL   Lower intermediate

RESOURCES   Make two copies of these prompt cards and cut them up into separate numbered cards. If you have more than 32 learners in your class, you will need two more sets.

1 a You were drinking orange juice …
  b … when you spilt it on your trousers.
2 a You were sunbathing …
  b … when it started raining.
3 a You were watching TV …
  b … and the power went off.
4 a You were having a shower …
  b … when the water went off.
5 a You were sleeping …
  b … and a mosquito bit you.
6 a You were chopping an onion …
  b … when you cut your finger.
7 a You were washing up …
  b … and you dropped a plate.
8 a You were smoking …
  b … and you burnt your shirt/blouse.

PREPARATION   Think through carefully how you can clearly mime the example sentences you will use in stages 2 and 3.

TIME GUIDE   40 minutes

Lesson

1 When you come into class, don't say anything. Go to the board and write, 'I have lost my voice.' Make a 'sealing your mouth' gesture to help make the point. Write 'Last night' on the board.

2 Stand in a place where everyone can see you easily. Mime the following and encourage the class to interpret your mime:

   I was playing tennis …

Ask them to give you the first part of the sentence, i.e. 'I was playing tennis …'. Mime playing tennis again and then mime:

… a tennis ball hit me in the eye.

Encourage the class to finish the sentence. If they don't use a connecting word, ask them which word would fit, i.e. 'when' or 'and'.

Write the whole target sentence on the board.

3 See if the class can guess some more mimes. Remember in each case to establish the past progressive activity first – before you introduce the second part:

You were swimming underwater   *… and found a pearl.*
You were travelling on crowded   *… when someone stole your*
bus …   *wallet.*

4 Invite a confident learner to come up to the front and try the next mime. Show him/her the first part of the sentence below and ask them to mime it to the class:

You were listening to a walkman …

When the class has got it, show the second part for the learner to do:

… and you fell asleep!

5 Divide the class into pairs and give out any two prompt cards to each pair – one card to each person. They shouldn't show their card to the other person. They should follow the same procedure as your example mime. When both mimes are finished the pair pass their prompt cards on to another pair and receive two new cards. The learners continue miming and passing cards until they have done all the mimes.

16 Making quizzes

TECHNIQUE   You give your class practice in listening to and making questions in the form of a quiz.

LANGUAGE FOCUS   Question forms in the past.

Pattern 1: The question word refers to the subject of the answer. In this case we do not use 'did' in the question, for example:

Who directed 'Star Wars'? – George Lucas.

Pattern 2: The question word doesn't refer to the subject of the answer, it refers to the object. In this case we use 'did' in the question, for example:

What did Shakespeare write? – He wrote plays.

LEVEL   Lower intermediate

RESOURCES   A quiz with 20 questions. You can use general topics or a specific topic that your class is interested in. You can also vary the difficulty of the questions. Here are two examples:

Pattern	Example question
Who wrote (book/play)?	*Who wrote 'Hamlet'?*
When did (something happen)?	*When did Picasso paint 'Guernica'? – 1937 or 1967?*

Prepare enough answer sheets for all the teams.

PREPARATION   Write your quiz. There are many different ways to organize a quiz. If there is a popular quiz programme on television, you may prefer to use that format.

TIME GUIDE   40 minutes

Lesson

1   Ask the class if they watch quizzes on TV or have done quizzes themselves. Ask what kind of questions are asked. Write your examples on the board and ask the class if they know the answers. Give them the answers if they can't guess them. Ask the class what topics are used in quizzes and write a list on the board, for example, History, Sport, Famous people, Film, Art, Geography, Science, Books, etc.

2   Organize the class into teams with about 5–6 people in. You can let learners choose their own teams, or in order to mix stronger and weaker students together, do it yourself. Here is one team-making idea:

Tear a piece of paper into small scraps. On each scrap write one letter of the alphabet. Use as many letters as you want to have teams, for example, use A, B, C, D, E, and F if you want to have 6 teams. Randomly distribute the scraps of paper (or make sure that certain people get certain letters). Tell the class 'All the As come to this part of the room – all the 'B's come here', etc.

3   Explain the main rules of the quiz:

Every team has one piece of paper. This is the Answer sheet. Write numbers from 1–20 down the left of this page. Each team must discuss every question. You must not write an answer until everyone agrees. There will be five questions in a round. At the end of each round, check the answers.

When everyone is ready, read out the first question. Allow some time for the team to discuss it and write their answer down next to number 1. Go on to questions 2, 3, 4, and 5 in the same way.

4   After five questions, ask teams to swap their answer papers with another team (who will mark it). Now go through the first five questions. Don't just tell them the right answer, but get them to think and explain their answers. Once or twice you may want them to look more carefully back at the question – so you could write one or two up on the board. Teams are awarded one mark for each correct answer.

5   When the papers are marked they should be handed back to their teams. Check which team is winning so far. You can now go on with the next five questions, and the next five, etc., up to question 20. Tell them, 'That is the end of the first half of the quiz ... but it's not over yet!'

6   If learners have not used Past simple questions before, spend a little time going over these, showing the two ways they are formed (see Language Focus at the start of the unit). Use your quiz questions on the board as examples.

7   Now ask each team to write five new questions with answers. When learners are writing their questions, go round and check that the questions and answers make sense and are true. Teams should write questions using both patterns.

8   When everyone is ready, continue the quiz. This time, team A asks their 5 questions first, and everyone can write answers (except team A of course). Go on till each team has asked their questions. The winning team is the one with most points at the end.

17 **Using real objects**

TECHNIQUE   You use real objects, or 'realia', to help explain a language point.

LANGUAGE FOCUS   'Used to' to talk about past habits and situations, for example, 'He used to read comics.'

LEVEL   Intermediate

RESOURCES   Two sets of objects. The items are all ordinary everyday items. Half the items should be old and represent former hobbies, sports, work, etc. The other half represent current hobbies, etc. Items could include:

Old items – 'used to'	*Current items – Present simple*
a bicycle pump	a spark plug (or other car part)
a comic	a newspaper
a tennis ball	a chess piece
a school exercise book	a class register
a map with town X	a map with town Y
a cassette	a CD

A flashcard of an adult

Two bags: an old-looking bag to keep the old objects in, and a modern bag for the new objects (optional).

PREPARATION   Collect the two sets of objects. Make sure they are separated into the correct bags.

TIME GUIDE   40 minutes

Lesson

1   Show the class a flashcard of an adult person and say his name, for example, 'Ramón'. Then show them the modern 'mystery bag', but don't show them the contents. Tell them that the contents belong to Ramón. Ask them what they think is in the bag. Listen to the suggestions but don't tell them if they are right or not. They must tell you about him. Pull out the first object, for example, the car part. Encourage learners to make a sentence about Ramón, for example, 'He drives a car' or 'He has a car' or maybe 'He is a mechanic'. Show the class the other items in the bag and ask them to make some sentences, for example:

He drives a car   *He's a teacher*
He lives in Manila   *He listens to classical music*
He reads newspapers
He plays chess

Put everything back in the bag.

2   Show the second bag. Explain that Ramón found the bag in his home yesterday. He hasn't seen the bag for 8 years! It is his own old schoolbag. It has things in it from the time when he was a schoolboy.

3   Put your hand in the bag and take out the first object, for example, the bicycle pump. Ask the class if they can say something about Ramón when he was young, for example, 'He had a bike', 'He rode a bike', etc. Explain that these are correct, but there is another way of talking about old habits or situations and write the beginning of the sample 'used to' sentence on the board:

He used to ...

Ask the class to finish the sentence using 'bike', i.e. 'He used to ride a bike' or 'He used to have a bike.' Now show them the spark plug and ask them to make the original sentence, 'He drives a car.' Finally ask them to put the two sentences together, i.e.

He used to ride a bike but now he drives a car.

4   Show the class the other items from the old bag and ask them to make some more sentences like the first, for example:

He used to	live in Vigan (map)		he lives in Manila (map)
	read comics (comic book)		he reads newspapers (paper)
	be a student (exercise book)	but	he's a teacher (register)
	play tennis (tennis ball)	now	he plays chess (chess piece)
	listen to pop music (cassette)		he listens to classical music (CD)

18 Turning lessons upside-down

TECHNIQUE   You help your learners use the target language before it has been 'taught'.

LANGUAGE FOCUS   Comparisons, for example, 'Tigers are bigger than rabbits'.

LEVEL   Elementary

RESOURCES   Simple pictures of animals. You could draw these on the board during the lesson or use pre-drawn flashcards.

PREPARATION   Practise drawing the animals.

TIME GUIDE   40 minutes

Lesson

1   Draw the animal pictures (or stick up the flashcards) at random positions around the board. Ask the class to copy the pictures in a similar random arrangement round their page. While they are drawing quickly check – and teach if necessary – the names of the animals.

Ask the class for some words to describe these animals. Using a separate column to the right of the board write suitable words up as they are said, for example, big, beautiful, funny, interesting, frightening, etc. You could add and teach a few new words yourself, for example, cute, intelligent, etc.

2   Draw a line connecting two animals, for example, lion and koala. Ask 'How are these two animals different?' Answer the question yourself by saying some sentences such as 'Lions are bigger than rabbits.' 'Lions are more frightening than rabbits' 'Rabbits are friendlier than lions', etc.

Don't 'teach' the grammar. As soon as learners understand the task, immediately ask them to work in pairs, doing the same as you did, drawing lines between animals and then describing as many differences as they can.

3   Monitor to check that learners understand what they have to do. Also notice what language they use (you could make some discreet notes) – but don't worry if they make mistakes.

4   Ask the class to tell you some of their interesting comparisons. If learners make errors with the target language in their sentences, for example, 'Snake more intelligent as mouse', repeat it yourself in a correct form ('Snakes are more intelligent than mice.'). If they don't include the target language, use examples yourself by:

a   making comparisons – 'I agree. I think snakes are more frightening than polar bears.'
b   asking comparative questions –'What do you think? Are snakes more dangerous than tigers?', 'Which are cheaper – ostriches or rabbits?'
c   eliciting comparisons – 'Tell me more about tigers and mice – what's the difference?'

Ask learners to repeat each correct sentence.

5   Ask the class to think of the examples they've heard and used. Then tell them to work in pairs for a few minutes to discuss how we make comparisons. As they are working write some hints on the board:

big	big	one syllable	-er
friendly	friend ly	two syllables	-ier
dangerous	dan ger ous	three syllables	more

6   To finish the lesson you could ask the class to think of one animal and make four or five sentences comparing their animal to four or five other animals. They then read out their sentences without saying the name of the animal and the class have to guess what it is, for example:

It's bigger than a dog.
It's smaller than a horse.
It's tastier than a snake.
It's softer than a cow.
It's more expensive than a rabbit.

(Answer: a sheep)

19 Listening and speaking

TECHNIQUE   You give the class an opportunity to hear the target language being used in different ways.

LANGUAGE FOCUS   Adverbs of frequency: 'always', 'often', 'sometimes', 'occasionally', 'hardly ever', 'rarely', 'never', ('once) a (week'), etc.

LEVEL   Elementary

RESOURCES   Chairs.

PREPARATION   Prepare the front of the class so that three people can talk comfortably and be seen by the rest of the class.
Think of possible questions and answers for the interview in stage 5.

TIME GUIDE   25 minutes

1   Tell the learners that they are going to watch a 'chat show'. If they are familiar with the idea on TV in their country, give a local example to make it clear what will happen. If they don't know the concept, tell them that a celebrity will be interviewed and the class will find out some interesting things about him/her. Explain that they can listen and enjoy it – just like a TV programme.

2   Ask them to get into groups of three or pairs and to think of about five questions starting with:

How often do you ...?

Write this on the board and ask for a few suggestions, for example, '... go to the cinema', '... have a haircut', etc. Explain that they can also ask follow-up questions.

3   Let the class prepare their questions. Walk round and monitor, noting the pairs or groups with the most interesting or amusing questions. Help if necessary. Set up three or four chairs at the front of the class so that the class can see. One chair should face the others.

4   When the class are ready, ask a group or pair to come to the front of the class and sit down. Sit in the chair facing them. Tell the rest of the class to make notes on your answers.

5   Ask the group or pair to ask you their questions. Answer as naturally as possible and at the same time give some clues about the meaning of the frequency words, for example:

LEARNER 1   *How often do you go shopping?*
TEACHER   *About twice a week. Usually on Saturday morning and once during the week.*
LEARNER 2   *Where do you go shopping?*

> TEACHER   *I always got to the local supermarket.*
> LEARNER 1 *How often do you go a restaurant?*
> TEACHER   *I don't usually go out to eat. I prefer to cook at home. But I probably go out about once a month.*

Make a note of your answers, making sure that you use a variety of adverbs.

6 When the interview has finished ask the class if they can remember any of your answers. Don't try to prompt them to use the frequency phrases at this stage.

7 Ask the class if any pair or group has any different questions. Tell them to come up to the front and go through the same process as stage 5. Depending on the size of the class and time you could repeat the process a few more times.

8 Tell the class to get into new pairs or groups and explain that you want them to think of five new questions of a similar type.

9 When they are ready ask for a volunteer to be questioned and a pair or group of interviewers. Tell them to come to the front and do the interview. This time make a note of the learner's answers. After the interview is over highlight the answers given and guide the learner to correcting their answer if they made a mistake, for example:

> TEACHER   *Can you remember your answer to the first question?*
> LEARNER   *'I go often to the cinema.'*
> TEACHER   *Good. 'I go often'. Can you change the order?*
> LEARNER   *I often go.*
> TEACHER   *Good. Try the whole sentence.*
> LEARNER   *I often go to the cinema.*
> TEACHER   *That's great. And how many times do you go to the cinema?*
> LEARNER   *Two times month.*
> TEACHER   *Twice a month.*
> LEARNER   *Yes. Twice a month.*

10 Ask for another volunteer and interviewers and go through the same process.

20 Asking concept questions

<table>
<tr><td>TECHNIQUE</td><td>You contrast the meaning and use of two language points by asking concept questions, i.e. questions about meaning.</td></tr>
<tr><td>LANGUAGE FOCUS</td><td>Talking about the future. Present simple, for example, 'The train gets in at 12.00.' Present progressive, for example, 'I'm meeting Olga at 8.30.'</td></tr>
<tr><td>LEVEL</td><td>Lower intermediate</td></tr>
<tr><td>RESOURCES</td><td>Four short dialogues:</td></tr>
</table>

A   Lily   *What time does the train arrive?*
     Givi   *Mmm. According to the timetable it gets in at 12.00.*

B   Givi   *What are you doing this evening?*
     Lily   *I'm meeting Olga at 8.30.*

C   Givi   *When does the film start?*
     Lily   *Let me see. Ah, yes. It starts at 9.35.*

D   Lily   *Are you cooking supper tonight?*
     Givi   *No. I'm having supper with Tengiz at a pizza restaurant.*

Concept questions, written on the board in a grid:

	A	B	C	D
1 Is the conversation about the present or the future?	future	future	future	future
2 Do we find the events in a time-table or a diary?	timetable	diary	timetable	diary
3 Were the events decided by one of the speakers or by someone else?	someone else	a speaker	someone else	a speaker
4 Can the speakers change the events or not?	cannot change	can change	cannot change	can change
5 Present simple or progressive?	simple	progressive	simple	progressive

<table>
<tr><td>PREPARATION</td><td>Divide the board into two halves. Write the concept question grid without the answers in columns A–D in the right-hand half of the board.</td></tr>
<tr><td>TIME GUIDE</td><td>30 minutes</td></tr>
</table>

1 Write dialogue A in the left-hand column of the board. Ask learners to copy it.

2 Point out the five grid questions. Ask learners to discuss each in pairs, noting their answers in column A, for example, if they think dialogue A is about the future they write 'future' against question in column A. Walk round and monitor to see if answers are similar to the sample grid above. Help if necessary.

3 When pairs have finished, ask them to do the task again for Dialogues B, C, and D.

4 Ask learners to study their answers and notice any general rules about how we use the two tenses to talk about future events. Discuss their conclusions with them and agree:

Dialogues A and C: We use the Present simple to talk about future events, often in a timetable, usually about things that the speakers did not decide and cannot change.

Dialogues B and D: We use the Present progressive to talk about events in the future that the speakers decided and can change. We don't usually find them in a timetable.

5 Dictate these sentences to the class. Say 'beep' for the blank parts. Ask the class to use their descriptions to help them fill in blanks with a suitable verb referring to the future.

1 I <beep> Pam for lunch.
2 The new term <beep> on September the fifth.
3 When <beep> Jack and Sally <beep> married?
4 The meeting <beep> at two o'clock.
5 They <beep> in a hotel for two nights.
6 I <beep> a party on Saturday.

21 Using example sentences

TECHNIQUE You use a selection of example sentences to highlight the meaning of a word and the patterns that surround it.

LANGUAGE FOCUS 'Get', 'got', for example, 'He got a letter from his girlfriend.'

LEVEL Intermediate

RESOURCES Example sentences

PREPARATION None

TIME GUIDE 45 minutes

1 Dictate the following sentences to the class, but say <beep> instead of 'got'. Tell the class to work in pairs to discuss which word is missing. Discuss the answer as a class.

1 He	got	*a letter from his girlfriend.*
2 They	got	*caught stealing a car.*
3 When he	got	*home he found his wife in the bathroom.*
4 I	got	*warm sitting next to the heater.*
5 He started losing his memory when he	got	*old.*
6 He didn't know he	got	*a pay rise every year.*
7 I	got	*back from France yesterday.*
8 My watch	got	*broken playing football.*

2 Ask the class to work in pairs again and to look for pairs of examples that are similar in some way. (Answers: 1,6; 2,8; 3,7; 4,5.)

3 Go through the answers with the class. Ask the class *how* the pairs are similar. There are two types of answer:

A—the basic meaning is similar:

Meaning 1 – 1 and 6 are similar to 'receive'
Meaning 2 – 2 and 8 refer to something that happened to something
Meaning 3 – 3 and 7 are similar to 'arrive'
Meaning 4 – 4 and 5 are similar to 'become'.

B—the pattern of words is similar:

Pattern 1 – In 1 and 6 'got' is followed by a noun (letter, bonus)
Pattern 2 – In 2 and 8 'got' is followed by a verb (caught, broken)
Pattern 3 – In 3 and 7 'got' is followed by a place (home, back)
Pattern 4 – In 4 and 5 'got' is followed by an adjective (old, warm).

4 Write the following jumbled sentences on the board and ask the class to put them in the correct order and identify the pattern.

get usually How school do you to?
your off Do you teacher get told by?
ever English Do during get you classes bored?
homework got you Have 100% for your ever?

(Answers: How do you usually get to school? (Pattern 3); Do you get told off by your teacher? (Pattern 2); Do you ever get bored during English classes? (Pattern 4) Have you ever got 100% for your homework? (Pattern 1))

5 Go through the answers with the class and then tell them to ask the questions to their partners.

22 Adapting written exercises

TECHNIQUE You liven up written exercises by adapting them to make them more communicative.

LANGUAGE FOCUS Time expressions: 'for', 'ago', 'until', 'while', 'from', and 'to'.

LEVEL Lower intermediate

RESOURCES Choose a typical written exercise from a coursebook, such as the following:

Fill in each gap with one of the following words: for, ago, until, while, from, to.

1 She bought the car six months _____.
2 I lived in Chicago _____ 1999 to 2003.
3 I was a footballer _____ seven years.
4 I watched TV _____ John wrote the letter.
5 We stayed in the disco _____ midnight.
6 I was an actor _____ two years.
7 I came to this town about four years _____.
8 I'm sorry we're closed. The office is open from 9 _____ 5.
9 I worked as a waitress in a small café _____ I was in New York.
10 I waited for you _____ 10 o'clock.

Pins or sticky tape.

PREPARATION Write out the 10 questions on 10 separate pieces of paper. Number each question.

TIME GUIDE About 40 minutes for all three exercises

Idea 1: making a new exercise

1 Write the words 'for', 'ago', 'until', 'while', 'from', and 'to' on the board. Ask the learners what they have in common (they are all time expressions, used to explain when things happened, started or finished, or how long they lasted.) Ask the class to think of some sentences that use one of these words in a time expression. Write two or three correct sentences on the board.

2 Erase the time expression word from each of the sentences on the board, replacing it with an underline. Point out that in this simple way, a sentence has become an exercise. See if they can remember what words to put back into the exercise to complete it.

3 Ask the class to make some new exercises themselves by working in pairs and writing three sentences each with a time word missing. Let the pairs work on their own, but walk round and monitor what they are doing, taking care to check that the sentences are correct and have the appropriate word missing.

4   When the pairs are ready they meet up with different pairs and exchange exercises.

Idea 2:
a 'wall dictation'

1   Take the pieces of paper you prepared before the lesson. Use pins or sticky tape to stick these up in different locations all around the classroom – and maybe even one or two outside the classroom (perhaps on a noticeboard).

2   Divide the learners into pairs. In each pair one learner is the 'reader', and the other is the 'writer'. The writer must take a new piece of paper and should make a list of numbers from 1 to 10 down the page. The reader's job is to go to any one of the question slips on the wall (it's not necessary to start at number 1), remember it (and its number), and then return to the writer. The reader should then tell the writer the sentence and the writer must write it down as accurately as possible next to the correct number. If the reader can't remember all the sentence correctly, or how to spell something, etc., then she/he must return to the wall and reread the text.

3   When one numbered sentence has been completed, the reader moves on to a different one and the task is repeated. After five sentences, writer and reader change roles. Make sure the learners don't shout out sentences across the room – that gets in the way of the reading, remembering, and spelling focus of the task.

4   When the learners have all the sentences copied down, they must work together to complete the exercise by filling in the gaps.

Idea 3:
'gallery feedback'

1   After all teams have finished stage 4 above, hand out some pins or sticky tape and ask the teams to make a 'gallery' of their answers along one wall of the room. In other words, each team sticks their answers on the wall (as if it was a painting in an art gallery).

2   Invite everyone to stand up and look at the answers. Ask the pairs to decide which sheet of answers has the most correct questions and answers. Give them a good amount of time to look around at all sheets and discuss with each other. When ready (and while everyone is still standing) collect feedback about their decisions, referring to the answer sheets for evidence and examples.

23 Auctioning sentences

<table>
<tr><td>TECHNIQUE</td><td>You use the idea of an auction to give your class practice identifying mistakes and correcting them.</td></tr>
<tr><td>LANGUAGE FOCUS</td><td>First conditional, for example, 'If you touch the dog, it'll bite you.'</td></tr>
<tr><td>LEVEL</td><td>Lower intermediate</td></tr>
<tr><td>RESOURCES</td><td>Write 10 sentences using the grammatical item you want to work on. Include a mistake in half the sentences. In the list below, sentences with errors are marked with an asterisk*:</td></tr>
</table>

1 If you will touch the dog, it'll bite you.*
2 If you give her the money, she'll give you her book.
3 Pete will annoyed if we're late.*
4 What will we do if it rains?
5 If you buy that bike, will you let me borrow it?
6 If you do that again was it bad for you.*
7 Mary thinks your football team are win if you play the match tonight.*
8 I'll phone you if you give me your number.
9 If you run quickly, you'll get there before the shop closes.
10 How get you home if there are no trains?*

<table>
<tr><td>PREPARATION</td><td>Cut up a number of pieces of scrap paper.</td></tr>
<tr><td>TIME GUIDE</td><td>20 minutes</td></tr>
</table>

....

Lesson

1 Divide the class into about 6–8 teams (fewer if you have a small class). Ask the teams to choose names for themselves and write these names up on the board. Allocate 300 units of local currency to each team by writing '300' under each team's name.

2 Write up the list of sentences on the board (without any indication as to which are correct or incorrect). Explain the rules to the learners:

—you are going to sell these sentences to them.
—half the sentences are not correct.
—the teams must try to 'buy' only correct sentences.
—the winning team is the one that has the most correct sentences at the end.
—you will give them 10 minutes to discuss and decide which sentences are correct, i.e. the ones they want to buy.

3 After the class has had time to study the sentences and make their decisions, say that you are going to start the auction. Explain briefly what an auction is by auctioning your pen, for example. Say that you will now sell each sentence on the board to the three teams that make the highest bids.

4 Introduce the first sentence and ask teams to write down on a piece of scrap paper the amount of money they want to pay for the sentence. If they think it's an incorrect sentence, they should bid '0' because they don't want it. They must also take care that they don't spend all their money on one item; they need to spend it evenly on as many good sentences as possible. When teams have all written down their bids ask them to hold up their paper in the air. Decide which three are the highest and award sentence 1 to each of them. Write the number 1 under each of the winning teams' names and deduct however much they spent from their original 300.

Team	A	B	C	D	E
	250	270	300	280	300
	(1)	(1)		(1)	

5 Continue with all the sentences, one by one. In each case 'sell' the sentence to the three teams that make the highest bids. When you reach the end every team should have bought some sentences.

6 Now go through the sentences one by one and ask the class to say which sentences are correct or not. If they are incorrect, they should correct them. For every correct sentence that a team bought add 100 to their total. Incorrect sentences earn nothing for anyone. The winning team is the one that has the most money at the end.

24 Revision ideas: putting the grammar back

TECHNIQUE You give your class a chance to revise a variety of language points and to practise their sentence building.

LANGUAGE FOCUS Revision of a range of sentence structures, particularly verb patterns and verb tenses.

LEVEL Elementary

RESOURCES Activity 1: a pointer, stick, or ruler suitable for indicating items on the board.
Activity 2: four keywords e.g. 'stop/lorry/policeman/say'

PREPARATION Activity 1: A set of about 20–25 words, parts of words and punctuation symbols suitable for combining together into sentences:

> what where did does is are has the
> and a magician rabbit to go want
> watch eat -en -ing ? . !
> you -ed -s -n't

Activity 2: Decide on the keywords. Choose keywords that can be combined in a variety of ways, for example, noun + noun + transitive verb would make a good set.

TIME GUIDE Each activity takes about 15 minutes.

Activity 1: Tapping

1 Divide the board in half. In the left half draw a large 'cloud'. Write the words (and pieces of words) in large letters in random positions within the cloud. Spread them out randomly in a mixed up jumble over the whole available space.

2 Stand at the board and ask learners to watch but not speak. Use the stick to tap words on the board, slowly one after the other, in the sequence of a sentence, for example, 'The magician watched the rabbit.' When you have tapped the whole sentence, ask the class to say the sentence.

If they make any mistakes, ask them to watch again and repeat the tapping. When the class can say the sentence correctly, ask someone to come up to the board and write the sentence on the right-hand side. Again check if everyone agrees – no spelling mistakes? word order problems? etc.

3 Do one or two more examples yourself. Here are some possible sentences:

What did the magician eat?	*The magician wanted to eat a rabbit.*
Where did the rabbit go?	*The magician watched the rabbits eating.*
Where does the magician go to eat?	*The rabbit and the magician are eating.*
Has the magician eaten the rabbit?	*Are you a magician?*

4 Learners work in pairs, study the words and find 3 or 4 other sentences they could make. Invite one person to come up front, take the pointer, and tap out their sentence.

Make sure they do it clearly and can be seen by the whole class. Ask the class to be quiet until the whole sentence is complete. Ask the class if they think the sentences are correct.

5 As the game goes on you should get a list of correct sentences on the right-hand side of the board. When you have finished ask learners to copy them into their books.

Activity 2: Rebuilding

1 Write on the board 'stop/lorry/policeman/say'. Explain to the class that they are going to make sentences by:

—adding words – only smaller 'grammar' words, i.e. auxiliary verbs, prepositions, articles, question words, conjunctions, etc.
—changing the form – for example, 'stop-stopping-stopped'.
—changing the order – for example, 'The policeman stopped the lorry.'

2 Do a first example sentence yourself. Then tell the class to get into pairs and think of about 10 new sentences. Walk round the class and help if necessary. When they have finished ask pairs to read out some of their example sentences, for example:

The policeman stopped the lorry.	*'Stop that lorry,' said the policeman!*	*'I couldn't stop the lorry or the policeman!'*
The policeman didn't stop the lorry.	*The lorry was stopped by the policeman.*	*Isn't that the lorry that was stopped by the policeman?*
That's the policeman who stopped the lorry.	*'Stop!' said the policeman to the lorry.*	*'Where's the stopped lorry?' said the policeman.*
Did the policeman stop the lorry?	*'Where's the policeman?' 'In the lorry.'*	*Who said the lorry was stopped by the policeman?*
The lorry stopped next to the policeman.		

25 Revision ideas: language puzzles, problems, and games

TECHNIQUE You can use these short language puzzles, problems, and games to get your class to review language they have studied.

LANGUAGE FOCUS Revision of items previously studied.

TIME GUIDE 5–20 minutes each. These games are quite flexible and will fit into different spaces in your lesson.

Idea 1: mixed up sentences

1 Prepare a sentence about 12–16 words long, using language that your class has studied recently, then mix the words up, for example:

you I feed my grandmother wanted to chickens phone asked me to the but

2 Divide the class into small groups. Write the words on the board and ask the class to see if they can find your original sentence using all the words. When a team thinks they have an answer go and check it – but let the other teams go on working. (Answer: *I wanted to phone you but my grandmother asked me to feed the chickens.*)

Idea 2: human mixed up sentences

1 This is the same idea again, but with one difference. Write each word from the sentence in large, clear letters, on a separate piece of paper, i.e. if there are 16 words there will be 16 pieces of paper.

2 Get 16 members of the class to come up front and stand in a line, from left to right. Give each of them one piece of paper in a mixed-up order. The task for the rest of the class is to find out what the complete sentence is. They can do this by asking each person their word and then rearranging the line. When they have made a new line, they can listen to the complete sentence and see if it makes sense. Do not say anything yourself. They should go on rearranging until they find a sentence they think is correct and then check it with you.

Idea 3: growing sentences

Write a short sentence on the board, including any language point you want to work on, for example:

I came home at five o'clock and found there was a party in my flat.

Under the sentence write 'Take 'party' – add three words'. Explain to the class that they must change the sentence by taking out one word and adding two or three new words.

I came home at five o'clock and found there was a very noisy disco in my flat.
(Take 'flat' – add two words.)

I came home at five o'clock and found there was a very noisy disco in my beautiful home.
(Take 'beautiful' – add two words.)

I came home at five o'clock and found there was a very noisy disco in my little country home.

You can play the same game in reverse – making the sentence shorter and shorter. Just change the rule: 'Take two or three – Put one'. How short can they make the sentence?

Idea 6: **100% gap fill**	**1**	Prepare a sentence using about 15–25 words, for example, 'Last Thursday evening I was feeling quite bored and so I went to the cinema and saw a really good detective film.' Carefully write the 'spaces' on the board for the whole sentence, for example, _ _ _ _ _ _ _ _ _ _ _ _ _ _ _ _ _ etc.
	2	Divide the class into teams. Ask the class to guess what the spaces represent – either words or letters In their turn, each team must guess either a letter or a word. Write in any correct guesses. Give one point for a correct letter and five points for a correct word. Continue till the sentence has been completed.

Techniques and lesson ideas

Unit 1
This technique gives the learners a chance to listen to and respond to language without having to produce it immediately.

Many other grammar points can be easily combined with imperatives, for example, countable and uncountable nouns – 'Tear out three pieces of paper', 'Pass him some paper'; prepositions of place – 'Lean the brush against the wall', 'Put the bucket under the table'; adverbs – 'Walk slowly to the door', 'Open the book nervously', etc.

Unit 2
Flashcards provide 'cues' that will encourage learners to say things. This may be when eliciting ideas about a story or perhaps when you want to do a quick drill and use pictures to prompt learners what to say.

They can be used to introduce and practise almost any language point – tenses, questions, comparisons, modal verbs ('have to', 'should', etc.).

Unit 3
Dialogues give learners clear examples of how we use language and interact with other people. They should also give a clear idea of the situation and the relationship between the people who are speaking, i.e. to put the conversation into 'context'.

Like flashcards, dialogues can be used for almost any language point. They are particularly useful for introducing language used in a given situation, for example, asking questions at a tourist information centre. Also for functional language, for example, requests, invitations, suggestions, offers, etc.

Unit 4
Pictures are a very effective way of introducing a situation – the characters and the location. The learners get a lot of information from pictures without having to know lots of vocabulary. It also gives them a chance to personalize the situation – give the characters names, say what's happening, etc.

Pictures can be used in this way for almost any language point.

Unit 5
Creating an imaginary situation can motivate learners by mentally taking them out of the classroom environment into a different location. This helps them to relax and communicate without worrying about their classroom personas.

Imaginary situations can be funny or unusual, both of which lead to better memorization, and can be used for a wide variety of language points.

Unit 6

In everyday life one person often knows something that another person doesn't know. We can visualize this as a 'gap' between people, an 'information gap'. A lot of conversation comes about because of such information gaps, and using them in class provides more realistic, natural, and motivating practice for learners.

Information gaps are often used for practising talking about the future – schedules, diaries, timetables, etc. They are also very useful for question forms, short and long answers, positive and negative answers, checking details, spelling, etc.

Unit 7

Role play can mean speaking 'as if you were someone else' or 'as yourself but in a different situation'. It can be used as a practice activity following a presentation of language – or as the task in an 'upside-down lesson' (see Unit 18). It can be a way to 'escape' the four walls of the classroom and expand the possibilities for practice.

This lesson demonstrates a very useful and adaptable way of setting up role plays for language practice. Using the role play 'preparation box' (rather than traditional role play cards) is a simple way to ensure that learners are clear about the context and the characters. It is reusable in future classes and can be used with a wide variety of language points.

Unit 8

In the presentation stage the diary is a simple and interesting way of showing that events are in the future. In the practice stage it creates an information gap that the learners need to fill by using tenses that refer to the future.

The diary idea works well for other tenses and grammatical items. Learners can practise the Past simple and Past continuous by talking about entries in a diary that refer to events before the lesson.

Unit 9

Stories, one type of reading text, provide lots of examples of language being used in context. The learners can also see how the language fits into the whole shape and structure of a story. This helps them to understand how the language is used. If the story is interesting, exciting, unusual, etc., this also aids memory. The lesson structure is based on the belief that learners must first be able to understand the meaning of a text before they can focus on the language points. For this reason, the questions are structured in this sequence: (a) general understanding of the text, (b) understanding of details, (c) personal views, (d) and finally the language focus.

Use reading texts to teach virtually any language point. Search for good texts, not just stories, but articles in magazines, pages from leaflets, notices, comics, etc.

Unit 10

Rather than teaching a new language item, this example focuses on comparing and contrasting items studied in previous lessons. Often a class that has studied some different grammar items may still be unclear on how they are formed or on differences of meaning. They may be unsure when to use which item.

Listening texts are very good for language used in everyday conversations.

Some other 'confusable' language items include: Present simple/Present progressive; Present perfect/Past simple; Past simple/Past progressive; modal verbs; passive and active forms; verbs that take a gerund/verbs that take the infinitive.

Unit 11

Questionnaires provide the basis for focused tasks with clear outcomes. They provide the learners with a simple and effective framework, and at the same time allow them to work at their own pace.

Questionnaires can be used with a wide range of language points: 'can'/'can't'; past, present and future time; different types of questions ('wh-', 'do'/'did', 'am'/'is'/'are', etc.). Learners can also design questionnaires themselves about topics they are interested in.

Unit 12

Telling a story is one of the most motivating ways to integrate grammar with listening practice. Learners always seem to like hearing about the teacher's life, especially if there are some 'secrets' in it. The prediction activity before the story helps learners to prepare for the listening stage.

Another variation is to tell the story in one lesson. The next lesson you tell the same story again. The following lesson you say you've forgotten some of the story and ask the learners to help you tell it.

Unit 13

Picture stories provide clues and prompts which stimulate learners to talk about connected past events. They contain information about the situation, the people, and objects which the learners can use to create their own version of the events depicted.

The 'writing robot' activity makes them think and be careful about language.

Picture stories can focus on the various past forms, adverbs – 'quickly', 'slowly', 'beautifully', etc.

Unit 14

Compared with traditional dictation (when a whole text is read and learners have to write it all down) this variation is focused more on grammar than on listening and spelling. The learners must think really hard to get the past verbs fitting logically and correctly into their story – and think not just about the form of grammar but also about the meaning and use of items. It's a challenging puzzle that really makes learners make use of what they know.

Unit 15

This is an excellent technique for getting learners to be more active in the classroom. Because the teacher takes a largely silent role, it allows the class to talk a lot more. It is demanding for learners as they have to interpret the mimes and think of the language they need. But it's also entertaining and hopefully the combination of challenge and fun will mean that the sentences are remembered for a long time after the lesson is over.

Mime can be used with a lot of activities including: describing present activities – 'He's eating a sandwich'; adverbs – 'She's walking slowly'; gerunds – 'Cooking is fun', etc.

Unit 16

The learners will be motivated to try and understand the questions and will worry less about any language problems they encounter. Learners will be exposed to a lot of the target language while receiving little explicit 'presentation'.

Quizzes are excellent for comparatives and superlatives, for example, 'Which building is taller: X or Y?', 'Which animal is fastest?', 'Which river is longest?', etc.

Quizzes are also good for descriptions of people and their lives.

Unit 17

Real objects bring an element of the real outside world into the classroom. Using the 'mystery bags' to reveal objects one by one helps to stimulate the learners' curiosity. Real objects also work well as cues for a drill. Once the items are known, you can indicate what sentence you want learners to repeat simply by holding up the appropriate object.

Modal verbs: Use the 'mystery bag' idea to reveal items the police found in a suspicious man's hotel room. Get the class to look at the objects and speculate about the man, for example, 'He might be a bank robber' (a pair of tights); 'He could be a cook' (a bag of flour); 'He must be a criminal' (a toy gun).

Narrative tenses: Tell a story of something that happened to you in the past and illustrate it by showing different real objects from the narrative. When you have finished help learners to retell the story by using the objects to remind them of the sequence of events.

Unit 18
Doing a task first allows you and the learners to judge whether there is a gap in their language ability. If there is, in the second stage of the lesson you can then help them 'fill in the gap' with explanations, practice activities, etc. It also helps motivation.

This technique can be applied to any language point by simply reversing the more traditional 'present first, then practise' order of the lesson.

Unit 19
This lesson includes a lot of useful listening work as well as focusing on a specific language area. The learners can hear a lot of target language being used naturally in a typical context. Work like this, although it seems less directly focused on single grammar items, is an essential part of grammar learning.

You can vary the list of questions you ask to include examples of specific language points, for example, referring to the future –'What are you going to do ….'; Present perfect – 'Have you ever …?', etc.

Unit 20
Concept questions, i.e. questions about the meaning of language, are important for checking if learners understand what you are teaching and finding out if they are with you or getting lost. They are more efficient than, 'Do you understand?' because the answer doesn't necessarily tell you anything. If a learner doesn't understand, they might still say 'Yes' because they are embarrassed, or maybe because they think they *do* understand. But with concept questions learners can prove they understand, and teachers can get accurate feedback from their class as to how they are doing.

Concept questions are usually worded so that they can be answered using short answers. They mainly use language that is simpler than the item they are checking.

Unit 21

This technique encourages learners to think about language problems from a variety of angles. It focuses mainly on getting learners to notice patterns of sentence construction, and also to realize that a common word, in this case 'got', can have many different uses.

Learners have to spot what item is missing from sentences, notice similarities in use, and work out reasons. Later they need to reorder words to make correct sentences. These activities focus them on thinking carefully about what is and isn't possible in English.

You could adapt this activity idea for many common words for example, 'make' or 'go' and almost any grammar point, for example, missing out the auxiliary verb in past progressive sentences or particles (short words such as 'up', 'out', etc.) in phrasal verbs.

Unit 22

Most teachers want their learners to do written exercises from coursebooks at some time. These tasks are often useful, but they sometimes need livening up.

Try this technique in future lessons with more complicated test types, for example, multiple choice, sentence transformations, etc., especially if you are preparing learners for an exam.

Unit 23

This technique is an entertaining game that has a serious teaching purpose. It encourages learners to think carefully about whether sentences are correct or not.

This technique works best for revision of previously taught items – although it is also good for language that they may have already met 'informally'. The 'first conditional' is a good example of this.

This technique works well with grammar where the meaning is relatively straightforward but there is often confusion over details of the word order or the verb forms, for example, passive sentences.

Unit 24

It is useful for a teacher to know a number of short activities that can be used to revise items learnt in previous lessons. The activities in this unit provide essential practice in using language. They raise questions as to what options are possible, which are impossible, and what the differences in meaning between the options are.

Because a large amount of discussion could arise, the time each activity might take is quite variable.

Both activities here are based on the idea of 'putting back' lost grammar. This challenges learners to review all the language they know in order to find possible structures.

Unit 25

Be careful when teaching that you don't only 'Input, input, input'. It's important that learners don't only get a constant stream of new items; they also need the chance to regularly go back and look over what has been studied, and have another go at practising these items. Most learners seem to understand and remember things only after repeated meetings and chances to try them out.

For this reason, revision lessons are vital, not just once a term, but often. Such lessons don't need to be boring; there are many ways to revisit previously studied items in activities that are still interesting and challenging. A simple way to revise is to regularly incorporate little games such as these into your normal lessons.

Glossary

Ways of organizing the learners in the classroom	Description
pair work	Each learner in class works with one other person so that everyone in the room can simultaneously get speaking practice. 20 pairs speaking at the same time gives 40 times more practice than if only one student is talking to the teacher.
small group	The whole class is divided into groups of three, four, or five people working together. Like pair work, this greatly increases the amount of learner talking time – and also allows each learner to hear a range of other opinions.
mingling	Getting the whole class to get up and walk around, as at a party, meeting each other and talking with different people, moving on when they need to.
whole class (also known as 'plenary')	The teacher works with all the class at once. Interaction is typically between teacher and one learner, but there is no reason why there should not also be a great deal of learner–learner interaction.
Aspects of a lesson	
lesson stages	Distinct separate parts of a lesson – each with a different kind of work and a different aim. A lesson might start with the teacher introducing a new grammar item (a presentation stage) and continue with an activity where learners try using the language themselves (a practice stage).
context	The situations we create in class for teaching purposes using pictures, dialogues, etc.
presentation	A lesson stage in which the teacher focuses learners' attention on language, for example when introducing new language, when clarifying features of previously met language, when giving information on aspects of form, meaning, pronunciation, etc., of items, or when organizing an activity or task that draws learners' attention to a specific language item, etc.
practice	A lesson stage in which learners get the chance to try using language items themselves. Practice may be 'restricted', i.e. the language they can use is limited to specific items, for example, a drill, or the practice may be 'authentic' when the learners are free to use any language they have at their disposal, for example, a discussion.
task	A task is something that we do, and we usually do things to achieve some desired result – buying a stamp in the post office, planning where we'll go at the weekend, and asking a friend if you can borrow their magazine. These are all tasks we do in real life. They

Glossary

	Description
	can all be mirrored in classroom activities, for example, making a plan for the weekend.
information gap	An 'information gap' is a task usually given to a pair of learners where each person has different information, or ideas, or opinions from the other. This leads to a need to communicate, passing the information from one to the other. A typical information gap would be when two learners have similar but not identical pictures and they have to work out, by talking only, what the differences are.
drill	Oral practice with very restricted language. In a simple drill the teacher says something and the learners repeat it. More complex drills may involve questions and answers or substitutions where learners must replace some words with others.
Teaching techniques	
brainstorming	Collecting a lot of ideas, for example, by naming a topic, for example, 'space', and writing up on the board every idea that people mention – 'alien', 'planet', 'rocket', etc.
eliciting	A technique for encouraging learners to speak more. The teacher aims to reduce his/her own speaking while increasing the learners' speaking.
	The teacher first gives some 'cues' such as a picture, a mime, a facial expression, a question, etc., and then tries to 'pull' language out from the learners. It's not a 'guessing game' – the teacher aims to provide everything necessary for learners to come up with the appropriate language. The teacher gives clear feedback, for example 'Yes', 'No', or nodding, so that learners know if they are correct or not.
	For example, in class instead of a teacher holding up a picture and saying 'This is Renaldo. He's a footballer.' She could instead elicit by showing the picture and asking 'Who is this?' and 'What does he do?' This simple change means that the learners will be the ones using the key language. A more confident teacher might even take this a step further by speaking even less, for example, just holding up the picture and gesturing that she would like the learners to speak about it.
monitoring	The teacher discreetly watches and listens, without interfering, to discover whether learners understood the instructions for a task, how effectively they are doing it, and the kind of errors they are making. Monitoring is mainly used when learners are working in pairs or small groups.

	Description
feedback	Information and opinions given by the learners to the teacher, for example, reporting on the outcome of an activity or whether they enjoyed it, or by the teacher to the learners, for example, evaluating how well the learners did a task, or answering 'Yes' or 'No' to learners' questions.
scaffolding	A technique to encourage a learner to speak by gently repeating, helping and almost invisibly correcting a learner's language while she speaks.

Teaching aids

flashcard	Pictures that the teacher can hold up to show the class. These are often used to elicit or as cues for drills.
cue	Things such as pictures, flashcards, gestures, etc., that will encourage learners to speak. For example, holding up a picture of a horse could be a cue to get learners to say 'horse' or 'it's a horse'.
mind map	A diagram (often of vocabulary items). These are not written in a traditional list form, but show connections between items.
time line	A diagram that can be used to compare the meanings of different tenses. There is an example in Unit 11, 'Making questionnaires'.